THE NIGHT OF AKHENATON

Ágnes Nemes Nagy

THE NIGHT OF AKHENATON

SELECTED POEMS

TRANSLATED BY
GEORGE SZIRTES

BLOODAXE BOOKS

ISBN: 978 1 85224 641 9

First published 2004 by
Bloodaxe Books Ltd,
Eastburn,
South Park,
Hexham,
Northumberland NE46 1BS.

www.bloodaxebooks.com
For further information about Bloodaxe titles
please visit our website and join our mailing list
or write to the above address for a catalogue.

Supported using public funding by
ARTS COUNCIL
ENGLAND

This is a digital reprint of the 2004 Bloodaxe edition.

CONTENTS

George Szirtes
INTRODUCTION

I have no doubt at all that Ágnes Nemes Nagy was one of the most important Hungarian poets of the post-war period. In fact I have no serious doubt that she is far more than this: that she is one of the great indispensible European poets of the twentieth century. This is a feeling I have had since first reading her in the 1980s. There was something crystalline and vast about the work, which imposed itself on me with all the authority of mountainhood. I felt it first, before understanding it, and if I now want to understand and explain it, it is because I am acutely aware that the reader, who may or may not be willing to take me at my word, will have only these and other translations as evidence. Translation is always a peculiar enterprise, but in the light of such claims it becomes a terrible responsibility. I would like to suggest that the meaning of that responsibility in this case is that whatever faults the reader is likely to find with my claim should be taken as the fault of my translations not the poems themselves.

That would seem to go without saying, but I bear in mind what Don Paterson says, in his Afterword to his versions of Machado, *The Eyes*. 'It should surely, by now, be axiomatic that poetry cannot be translated in a way that will preserve anything of the flavour of the original. Poems are custom-built churches in which the poem's own voice…can sing freely; but one so specifically calibrated to maximise the resonant potential of that voice, that another voice, upon entering the same space, is almost guaranteed to fall flat.' He also warns that reading a poet 'through the lens of his or her biography' is as pointless as trying to 'explain' a poem 'in terms of a geographic or psychological provenance'.

Paterson is both right and wrong. He is right in stating certain truths about poems. He is right if he means that poems make their own, unreproducible voice, and that they are not to be read as symptoms of various conditions, whether these conditions be geographical, historical or psychological in nature. He is wrong, however, if he means that the poem's voice exists without its interpretations, interpretations that have various notions and expectations of what constitutes a church, and if he means that poems can be entirely abstracted from their conditions: on the contrary, it is partly because they contain those conditions that they mean anything to us.

In the case of Nemes Nagy, the essay reproduced here (87-94), one written by herself, in 1980, would seem to confirm Paterson's argument. 'All poetry is untranslatable. Hungarian poetry is even more untranslatable,' she tells the reader in the course of the introduction to a volume of translations from her own work. I will not point out the obvious paradox, which speaks for itself, but will complicate it by adding that she herself, like most Hungarian poets, had translated a considerable volume of poetry from other languages into Hungarian.

Rather than engaging in a theoretical debate about what constitutes a poem and what constitutes a translation, I want to return to my first sensation, which is in itself a kind of poetic image: the crystalline mountain. Why crystalline? Why a mountain? I want to begin to answer these questions by defining crystals and mountains.

The dictionary tells me that, among other things, a crystal is 'a clear transparent mineral', and that it is 'an aggregation of molecules with a definite internal structure...a solid whose constituent particles are symmetrically arranged'. So, what I seem to mean, is that there is something both highly clear and highly structured in the experience of reading her poems. There is nothing particularly difficult or cloudy in the words themselves, and the formal structures − metrical, rhyming, employing logical antithetical statements − are equally obvious. They govern the nature of saying. This does not mean that the clarity is itself the poem: as with a crystal there is an awareness of refracted light, of light held and turned about various facets. But there is, nevertheless something epigrammatic, gnomic, almost absolute about the manner, about the mind itself.

A mountain is defined as 'a large natural elevation of the earth's surface rising abruptly from the surrounding level'. The elements of largeness, naturalness and abruptness, figure importantly here, nor can we quite forget the base, the bottom line: the earth. We are not used to thinking of formality as natural, indeed one might be forgiven for thinking, after reading some writers, that form and nature were antithetical. But what could be more natural than a crystal? Nemes Nagy's poetry is full of images of nature as structure: of rocks, of levels, of layers, of molecules. The sheer largeness also strikes us as natural. It is partly a largeness of subject matter, meaning geography, geology, enormous wills and powers rather than epic battles or voyage, and partly a largeness of what is constantly present but rarely referred to in personal terms: history, the power of states, of impositions, of moral demands and of obligations. As for the abruptness, this is visible partly in the curtness of the epigrammatic

8

forms, and partly in the rational dislocations of the more narrative and prose poems.

None of this is cuddly. Nemes Nagy will never appeal to the tender, sweet or maternal aspects of the imagination. There are many reasons a poet might have for rejecting, as Nemes Nagy did, the term 'woman poet' and this could be one of them. There is little, if anything, of the received notion of the feminine in her. There is an early poem, 'Thirst', which is not included here, that articulates a fierce sexuality, but she was just as fierce in her demand that the poem should be left where it was, untranslated. This demand was part of the absolute element in her person, and is perfectly consistent with absolute elements in the poems. Her sense of the female, as opposed to the feminine is explored in one poem that is included, 'Female Landscape' (18), where she talks of how 'thought flowers from my shoulder / with its stout unfurling bud'. And it is in fact 'thought' that in the poems, appears to be central to her, from which we might conclude that she is an intellectual poet *tout court*. In her essay, on the other hand, she talks about the poet being 'the specialist of emotions...the duty of the poet [being] to obtain citizenship for an increasing horde of nameless emotions'. These emotions in Nemes Nagy burst steaming out of the ground of her being as does the hot spring in 'Geyser' (34), but the light whereby we perceive the spring, and the emotions, has passed through the crystal of the intellect, which is as fierce as the emotions themselves. In the 'Dialogue' (42) between the flag and the flag-pole, it is the flag-pole that reminds the fluttering flag of the true relationship between them:

– Let go of me, flagstaff! Why cling on to me?
– You're merely rag, dear flag, till you belong to me.

It is the pole, not the flag. It is the earth, not the dancer; the mountain not the mountaineer. I once told the late Ottó Orbán – himself one of the major poets of the second half of the century, and quite as volcanic a figure – that I thought of Nemes Nagy's poetry in terms of mountains. He told me he had once danced with her at a party: 'And believe me,' he said, 'it was like trying to dance with a mountain.'

I started visiting Nemes Nagy in 1985 and saw her regularly until her death in 1991. She lived in a darkish flat in Buda, by Joliot-Curie Square, her window open to the doves who would perch on the sill. Her reputation was daunting, a quarrelsome, difficult figure: some referred to her as 'the lion', others as 'the witch'. I was lucky in that she was interested in me, perhaps in the odd literary phenomenon I represented. In any case I sensed the lion but was never aware of the witch: I took it as a symptom of rejection or criticism and the malice of the person rejected or criticised, but also of her power. We met and talked for an hour or two each time, in Hungarian. I would bring flowers. She would serve black coffee and some nibbles and we would talk around a low table. On the wall was a portrait of a beautiful, brooding young woman with long blonde hair. It was her, painted just after the war, or perhaps during it. This was the young woman, who, together with her then husband, the critic and literary scholar Balázs Lengyel, started a new magazine, called *Ujhold* ('New Moon'). The magazine attracted the best of the poets and novelists of the immediate post-war period, picking up where the most important inter-war Hungarian literary magazine, *Nyugat* (or 'West') had left off. Its face, like *Nyugat*'s, was set toward Western Europe, the world of subjectivities and systems: Freud, Rilke, Eliot, Montale, Seferis, Ionesco, Beckett (Beckett as he was to develop in the 50s). It was not a face that could survive the Stalinist takeover of 1949. The magazine was banned, its contributors silenced or imprisoned: Lengyel, for one, was imprisoned; Nemes Nagy, for one, was silenced. She found work as a schoolteacher. She wrote some still-popular books for children and translated poetry out of other languages. The brightly blazing project that had emerged from the darkness of the war had been snuffed out in its infancy. Lengyel too, it turned out, had been unfaithful to her, so when he emerged from prison she threw him out.

Betrayal was everywhere. Betrayal stiffened her resolve and gave her energy. It was partly betrayal that grew into the great crystalline mountain; betrayal that powered the hot springs. It is the theme of betrayal that runs like a high-voltage electric current through the short poems of the 'Journal' sequence. It is that which burns forever the 'low flame' of 'unquenchable bitterness', it was why 'no judge' would dare try her, why she feels scorn for Thespis whose character changes with her make-up. Nemes Nagy's belief is not in people but in the forces and structures of nature that not only supply the missing moral dimension in human life but surpass it by mysterious moral laws of their own. So the tree in 'Trees' (16), a key poem for her, offers a lesson in steadfastness and survival; so the ninety-two elements in 'Above the Object' (52) stand, wearing their own curious caps of light; so the morning develops its own theology in 'Hemisphere' (59): this is why the forces of the earth, those 'hot horses of earth and clay' in 'The Sleeping Horsemen' (58) can 'strain upward with their leafy hair, / and with one slow enormous leap / gallop away'.

This mystical element is noted in the excellent commentary provided by Hugh Maxton for the book of his own translations of Nemes Nagy's poems, *Between* (Dedalus Press, Dublin, 1988), of which more in a moment. Maxton notes the instability of Nemes Nagy's poetic geology and remarks on an 'impatient questioning of an otherwise untraceable God' and a religious sensibility that 'strikingly lacks a potential present, confronting instead spiritual redundancy and infinitely postponed renewal'. What he detects is an affinity with Beckett that Nemes Nagy herself saw and claimed. He tells the reader of her background, that she was born in 1922, to a professional family of Transylvanian descent, and that she numbered 'several Calvinist ministers among her forebears'. There is, or so Maxton appears to be hinting, a sense of God's presence in his absence. Maxton's translations flesh out his surmise. I have found them invaluable and, sometimes, beautiful, though this book will appear to represent a clear argument with his.

It is the nature of translations to argue: the true voice that Don Paterson talks about is, to a substantial extent, the voice of that argument. The voice is in there, echoing somewhere among its hearings. Or, to adopt a strand of Maxton's argument, the place where the voice is absent defines the position of the voice. My own quarrel with Maxton – my relocation of his echo – is not about his presentation of the mountain but of the crystal. His translations of poems that deal directly with nature, poems such as 'Between' (29), 'Hot Water Spring' (my 'Geyser', 34), and 'Night Oak' (54) are impeccable. Powerful, rhythmically compulsive, they were very hard not to steal from. I had to keep averting my eyes from them. My versions of poems such as these are not a world away from his; they are more or less the next field. We could shift the hedgerow or wind-break a foot or so either way, but the soil is the same.

Not so, where the poems are crystalline. At the end of his commentary Maxton defines Nemes Nagy as 'both classicist and avant-gardist'. It is the classicist that we view wholly differently. We may be observing the same object but we see it from different planets. Where he sees mystery and enigma, I see light and shape. Or rather, I see a foreground of light and shape, with mystery and enigma as functions of shape and light. There could be few more striking contrasts than between Nemes Nagy's 'Napló' (19), the poem that

11

Maxton titles 'Diary' and I call 'Journal'. This contrast informs many other poems, particularly those where Nemes Nagy is pursuing a line of thought. Nemes Nagy's own view of the role of the intellect is there in 'Nightmare' (19):

> From a world of rotting rags and clout
> The marsh-light of cold reason flashes out,
> Plays on the corpse, the softening skull beneath,
> And illuminates its naked row of teeth.

But then 'Nightmare' is one of the poems from the 'Journal' sequence, and the lines above are in my translation. Not surprisingly, my translation agrees with my view of its translation. It is not for the translator to recommend his own wares, nor would I in fact be wanting to seem to do so, even at second hand. The voice is not in either side of the argument: it is in the argument itself. It is – to return to Don Paterson – the echo from the other end of the church that sets the ambience for echoes to come, echoes that I feel sure will come, if only because I am certain that Nemes Nagy will continue to invite them.

It is tempting to end here, and not to engage with Paterson's distractions of 'geography and psychology'. I myself am more than willing to leave the psychology to the reader. Nor do I want to impose an unwieldy engine of footnotes or other scholarly apparatus on what seems to me self-singing and self-explanatory. The earlier poems in the book – which is set out chronologically, the poems appearing in the order in which they appeared in the order of the books – are clearly to do with survival; with fear of bombs and bullets during the war and of surveillance and arrest after it. That is what the poems down to 'Notes on Fear' (22) take for subject and attempt to resolve, often by reference to interiors rather than nature or the idea of nature.

Nature appears as a disturbing force covering up history in 'Balaton' and expands to become the central disruptive energy in poems like 'Between' (29) and 'Statues' (31). Statues are potent images in Nemes Nagy: they signify human ambition, human identity, the incomplete order of the intellect: they are broken, one sinks under their weight, they are erected as substitute gods in the Akhenaton poems, they appear phantasmally in the prose poems. They are an insupportable moral burden. They are undermined by the wild heart of the hot spring in 'Geyser' (34), where time nails the silver gush into 'steam and frozen emptiness', so water and energy themselves become a statue. The shorter poems, such as 'Lazarus' (35), 'Alcohol' (37) and 'Breath' (38) attempt to embody other compulsive energies in compact sculptural form: a corpse, a drink, the space between two physical bodies. There are indeed contrary desires, one for the intellectual and spiritual to leap free of its material prison, the other for the feckless, weightless fluttering of the spirit to root itself in something, if nothing else then in atoms, molecules, grains of light; to have 'a building plastered down with sky' as the poem 'Wind' (43) has it, and yet to be free of the spirit, as of the terrible creature in 'Bird' (44) that squats on one's shoulders, without which one would 'topple over like a log / If he were now to up and go'.

The Akhenaton poems are where Nemes Nagy grapples most intensely with history, responsibility and justice. Here she tries to carve a theology or cosmology out of these desperately fissile forces. She identifies with the boy God-King: she looks to invent a necessary god; she recalls the energies of the 1956 Uprising and tries to find rituals to articulate them; writes short memos to herself about the nature of a possible godhead, and constructs a kingdom of objects and phenomena. Feelings of yearning and extraordinary pride (Akhenaton, after all, made himself into a god) undergo an intellectual self-examination that turns them into powerful and, in my view, unforgettable symbols. The verse – and in these poems I diverge from Maxton – remains deeply formal and restrained: the wild, wild thought is carved into large, clear rational forms. It takes a mighty flagpole to support such an enormous flag.

Some of Nemes Nagy's most powerful poems follow the Akhenaton cycle. The dynamic of balance between nature and intellect, between energy and form is at its strongest. 'Night Oak' (54) doesn't just deliver a lesson, like the earlier 'Trees' (14), but actually gets up and walks (Maxton and I are fairly close here); The Sleeping Horsemen are both earth and energy. In the already mentioned theology of 'Hemisphere' (59)

> ...one dark half hangs on and aches
> like a black cauldron under the great lakes.

In 'Spectacle' (60) the inside of the whole skull is like a circular screen; the walls are 'bright knives, furniture'.

The prose poems, which are at the most 'avant-garde' edge of Nemes Nagy's work, enable the great flag of the imagination to run across familiar landscapes of streets and museums, no longer controlled by verse form but by syntax alone, a highly prosaic, deliberately dry syntax of reportage, footnotes and field notes. They are visionary scenes in which worlds run into each other and explain themselves in each other's terms Their mystical, surreal, intellectual dislocations are nevertheless an attempt to discover a valid structure, the principle that holds things together. They are extraordinary excursions into almost regimentally disciplined freedoms.

The late poems after that were mostly unpublished. Nemes Nagy was not a voluminous writer. She wrote books of essays, saw *New Moon* re-established by younger poets after 1986, but kept her poems to herself. Many of them were about her own illness and approaching death. She was always too distant, too unbending, too disdainful of popularity to be a popular writer, but was at the same time acknowledged to be of the first importance. Her readings of her own poems are available on commercial records which do not yield much to drama or histrionics: the voice is sharp and firm, stating rather than singing. It is the poems themselves that sing. She has exerted lasting influence on poets coming after her: on Zsuzsa Rakovszky, on Gyozo Ferencz and on Mónika Mesterházy. To some degree it is a moral influence as much as a matter of range or technique, something to do with integrity, with what Hugh Maxton rightly regarded as 'intellectual passion'. It is also, I think, to do with crystalline clarity in a world that tends to smoke and obfuscation, and with the building of mountains on deeply treacherous soil.

I can't walk into the Nemes Nagy chapel of Don Paterson's church and make the same noise as she does, but I can try to put down what I hear, as I hear it, and hope to hear it again as I mouth these words. I have been working at these poems, on and off, for some 16 years: I don't imagine they are finished, or that they are all they might be in themselves. As echoes, however, they may draw attention to the church that she has made her own, which is a remarkable cathedral of air, both crystalline and mountainous, and from whose heights the 20th century may be seen marching away below.

GEORGE SZIRTES

Trees

It's time to learn. The winter trees.
How head to toe they're clad in frost.
Stiff monumental tapestries.

It's time to learn that region where
the crystal turns to steam and air,
and where the trees swim through the mist
like something remembered but long lost.

The trees, and then the stream behind,
the wild duck's silent sway of wing,
the deep blue night, white and blind,
where stand the hooded tribe of things,
here one must learn the unsung deeds
of heroism of the trees.

EARLY POEMS

Female Landscape

A lie of land so yielding, gentle,
you want to stroke it, see it break.
Between its knees the broad stream flows
glittering like a curious snake.

Dense valley, luxuriant hill
gentled under aeons of praise –
this female landscape loses me:
what can I do but stand and gaze?

The Baltic Sea has bathed her feet,
tyrrhenian foam has washed her hair,
but her smooth navel makes me think
of quite another place, elsewhere,

where tortoises are being taught,
where life grows taller and the dim
heat sucks scarlet flowers from
the giant spiky cactus limb,

where children ride mosquitoes, where
neither light nor reed is blunt,
where all is bladed as the mind,
and hot as any hothouse plant,

where honey-thick, yet thicker still,
juice drips down the moss of trees
and in the pond cool greenish stars
pulse against my calves and knees,

where the lobster slops and burrows
through mud hotter than any mud,
and thought flowers from my shoulder
with its stout unfurling bud.

from Journal

Mind

I know I have no reasonable grounds
for thinking, but watch the thoughts as they go round.
And since contempt's appropriate to the act
mindlessly I trust to intellect.

Nightmare

From a world of rotting rags and clout
the marsh-light of cold reason flashes out,
plays on the corpse, the softening skull beneath,
and illuminates its naked row of teeth.

Revenge

He who cannot take revenge,
nor yet forgive, must find redress
in burning for ever the low flame
of his unquenchable bitterness.

Sic Itur ad Astra

Compare with these I am a saint
            no judge would dare try me;
if the world wags on like this
            they will deify me.

July

Light and light and sunspots, fragrant colours,
in place of my heart, *de rigueur* – bouquets.
Just this once, dear world, I will forgive you,
but from now on you'll have to mend your ways!

You sit and read

You sit and you read. How alone you are, even you don't know.
But sometimes you guess and then with a leisurely movement
and a hint of mild animal sadness your simple features
dip into the light.

Before the mirror

You take your face and slowly remove the paint,
but would remove the face that fate assigned you,
you wait for the armchair to rise and with a faint
gesture of boredom to appear behind you.

Contemplative

The old pose lost its charm. Let's take
a new one out. Yes, this will do.
In matters of dress it's all the same
what you fit your body to.

The dress, the body and the soul,
the same applies to everything.
When Thespis prinks does she at all
suspect what change the colours bring?

Sincerity

Inspecting myself makes me bilious.
It's easier for the spontaneous.
I would if I could be the driver of the dray
who washes great blond horses all the day
and has nothing to say.

No wish

No wish to die, no, none at all
though days stack up in bitterness
against me now, despite their gall
my thirst remains and hurts no less.

Oh, I could rest, my eyes replete.
A tall tower held me, while outside
the night, a hundred metres wide,
trampled the sea with its loud feet.

I strolled down wooden avenues,
heard subterranean gusts below,
passed corners of corridors; would cruise
electric-lines where tramways go.

The snow in Rome once fell like this –
we crossed the Mura on poor brutes
like Sultan, our pony-Pegasus,
with hand-grenades, mess-tins, army boots.

I buried Germans, corpses, bare...
saw the provisional government,
the ruined house where love was spent,
I dread, but dread's nor here nor there.

I have grey hairs. Spring wind blasts through
the tangled, wild hair of the world.
In vain, I say, but vain's the word
since desire stirs in me too,

desire for breath, a breathless call
to life alone, to hunger – sky
is changeable, clouds drive and fly –
no wish for death then, none at all.

Notes on Fear

Why should I care if it is dumb or shrill –
whatever it does to me, it cannot kill.
And even if I trembled like a leaf
I doubt I would entirely come to grief –
death, if it comes, comes not by its will.

*

Ah but the pain, the bodily pain,
the splintering bone –
those who nature herself has robbed
of life, they too whimpered and sobbed,
transfusion-bruised and mottled they
opened their blotched arms to pray –

It's all the same then. Same? Disgust
at burdens the mind self-inflicts:
to fend off death's hawk-hovering
by seeking death as covering.

*

The helpless can tremble, right enough!
A mobile fleshy plant, man hides
beneath closed petal-veils, the rough
freight that haunts his frail insides;
between curved ribs the fluttering heart
shivers and quivers like the clock
by which he measures his hourly stock,
and though he barely seems to flinch,
not as you'd notice, pinch by pinch,
the air vibrates invisibly
with heart's suppressed fragility.

*

Take breath and gulp the air. Breathe in
the dusk of spring so full of space.
The windows, brilliant, Easter-bright,

dazzle with evening, drop by drop,
as with a pinch of spice, held tight
and undistorted in the glass.

Tenements: vague shifts of light.
A neon-sign observes po-faced
sparks from a forge create a chaste
shrunken Ur-maternal flare.
At the foot of the fire-wall a hut
opens its tin door on the square;
nearby, a pale horse vaguely lumbers,
its great mane flickering with embers.

Over in the park, still bare,
the lately-planted saplings drowse.
Your eyes ascend along the boughs
and notice how it's not yet night:
the sky is green, pink-velvet tipped,
ebony-rods of bald twigs scrawl
close letters in an unknown script,
and there in one green slice of sky
the pole star sparkles like live coal.

*

Inside, a clutch of tulips blow.

Like someone caught out in a storm,
drenched and ruffled and windtorn,
like fevered heralds stammering out
an agitated message they
embody rather more than say,
their very loveliness appears
by the good grace of pinking shears,
of blade and hand and shop display
but break through impenetrable mesh,
the protective cordons of the flesh,
the heart's panicky measures, quick
as the hand's protective flick:
they shock my eyes, they hiss and shake
like lightning breaking on a lake.

Don't toy with me, earth – it was you,
mother of worms, that gave them birth!
They're your creatures, no excuses,
this immoral drama that produces
or reduces us is simply what you do.

And you too there, with your dumb gaze,
your silver-spoked eyelids quite unfazed,
you watch your million children thrash
in the hot wind, strewn like ash.

BALATON CYCLE

Balaton

1

A skimpy cotton bathing-suit
marks her out as of our age,
her small breasts shimmer like a cute
Naiad's among the foliage,
her dark head lost in stumpy reeds,
her still neck gently dandled by
brief ringlets. Her arm moves through weeds.
To lay observers she might seem
a new Ophelia of the stream.

The boy arrives, thrusts out for her.
Faint curls of blond hair on his tanned
thighs bend before the rushing water
which presses against leaf and hand.

2

Who'd believe the surfaces
of Balaton, above, below,
were underwritten by the skeins
of dead men, wrecks, old aeroplanes?

A marshy lake. Moon trickles down
into her like sugar-cane,
half boiled away at noon
in some southerly terrain,
only in autumn, when water clears
will you note the rising steam
touching the hill's crown and see where shapes
of gentler gods are nourished by
nanny-goat dugs of dangling grapes.

3

The smaller lake behind the long
promontory. This slender
water was once part of the greater.
Geology in fields of lavender.

It kneads at hills, tears things apart,
turns sand to humus and its vast toes
protrude monstrously
from earthen shoes.

4

How warm the boards are. They
practically steam when a head
of water strikes them. Take off that straw hat
and cover your face with it instead.

The plank beneath your ear is like a drum.
Water drums faintly under its skin.
Dense reeds hold the sound, hearing
The boards crack again and again.

Sleep on, angler. It's precisely three,
the hour when Christ died. Sun glides
unobserved across the lake,
notes its double image and divides.

5

Nor moon, nor way. Looking up, the eye
meanders through star-thickets in the sky.

Still visible below, a stone ledge, luminous,
as if coated in pure phosphorus.

Brushing the hill's bosom, your hand scrapes
on swollen udders of wild grapes.

The wonder is the sky does not ignite
with all its marvels in its self-delight!

And terror – sky reflects on how it might
Manage when it's time to end the night.

6

Copper-red and grey
have plunged daggers into
each other: twilight is in turmoil,
the broad air of the sky trembles.
But does not move, trembles:
twin hues rumble, the foam
endures, until it leaps:
the lacerations of the storm.

7

Wind bites but lake endures, while dusk
struggles on, no moon tonight –
so none shall see, conceal your face
under the very lack of light,
the girl is dead, so none shall see,
concealed in slackening reeds and slime
but tide's too thin, her back floats up,
no depth there but in terms of time,
a marshy lake mud serves to warm,
steam rising, boards too hot to bear,
cover your face up for your lot
is beauty and terror everywhere,
bosom, grape-cluster, girl-foam: sun
flicks its whip, card cracks, a wedge
of monstrous footprints lead you to
swollen udders beyond the edge
of the north shore while night beguiles
with thickets of stars, how can our pride
let it end, no vision, no moon,
this very hour at which Christ died.

Between

The air's enormous empty sleeves.
Air supporting birds and the whole panoply
of bird-lore, ornithology,
wings on fraying winds of argument,
the unpredictable, inconsequent
boughs that a moment of sky relieves,
trees of living mist, spiralling desire
to the topmost branches,
breathing, twenty to a minute at a time,
vast angels barnacled in rime.

The mass below. The plain with mounds
of earth, juddering, huge, immovable,
where ridges and hump-backed cliffs lie down
or kneel – geography's sculpture hall –
the vale a moment of forgetfulness where
attention wanders, and then more
masses and forms from skeletons of lime bone
to the far perimeter, a single core
of being, crumpled into stone.

Between the earth and sky.

Explosions in deep mountain bores.
Meanwhile the sun's transparent ores
turn stone to metal, almost to themselves,
and when beasts walk across them, their claws smoke,
and smoke-ribbons of burning hoofs
wind round and round above the cliffs' sheer roofs,
till night falls on the desert plain,
night that quenches and extends into the tight
core of what was stone, sub-zero night,
among the splitting and collapsing
of cartilage, joint, flagstone, sett,
flexed in an endless
decimating unconsciousness
by white and black quotidian
lightning flashes without sound –

Between the day and night.

Those decimations and incisions,
droughts and visions,
inarticulate resurrections,
the unbearable vertical tensions
between up-above and down-below –

Various climates and conditions.
Between. The stone. The tracks of tanks.
A line of black reed on savannah border,
written on pond and sky in lines, in double order,
two dark stones with cryptographs
stars' diacritics, acutes and graves –

Between sky and sky.

Statues

Bitter.
            Bitter the ocean when I rolled
down the cliff's throat, a pebble stumbling
down spiral stairs, and as I fell
I heard the empty shell
like memory in an empty house behind me humming,
and I rattled
like loose metal, shrapnel in the skull.

Then tumbled out across the beach
to find the statues.

There, on a sculpted base
a turtle's egg with its own carapace:
my skull simmering in heat of day,
my white helmet rolled away,
a tiny bubble in the sand,
I lay, my shoulders against the cliff's broad foot
filthy, filthy in my stained white suit.

            Whose is this block?
            Who was it who from this mountain of slate
            furiously carved an extraordinary state
            of indifference out of rock?

And tin, small shards of tin all over me,
buckled tin cans, metal panes
that, stuttering, beat back the light,
brilliant as the wreck of a downed plane,
something still living moving within,
a watchstrap, bloodstained,
I lay there spread against the cliff
an animated filth laid over stone.

            No one more stubborn than you, none,
            you who cast yourself in stone,
            into object, into stone
            your live neck and backbone,
            this is an age of stone, an age,
            a blind life of diminished sense.

Who carved out such indifference?
Who was it carved that living weight
of neck out of this heap of slate?

Salt and sand, the mass of rock above,
cave carved in sky,
this relative eternity
these minerals in twilight dress –

the sea booms out, one Earth its bed:
a stone bowl for its bitterness.

Statues I carried

Statues I carried on board,
vast faces unnamed and unspanned.
Statues I carried on board
to the island where they should stand.
Between nose and ear there were ninety
degrees, measured precisely,
with no other sign of their rank.
Statues I carried on board,
and so I sank.

Geyser

It began. First came the salt.
The crystals split and then
reformed. So it began. Earth's icy feet
trod all things down and ground them deep.
Then came the voids. Grown slender,
subjected to enormous pressure,
it gradually squeezed between
the tortured folds of rock below,
till suddenly: echo,
a whole precipitous caveful of it, then once again
the cranial black shell
of an enormous stony brain,
cut into clod and runnel
in scalding corkscrew motion, to strain
and steam until –

It burst. Suspended, still.
One long vertical sliver
of time nailed into steam and frozen emptiness.
The leap itself pure silver,
all watery muscle, bodiless,
a stretching forth, helpless, stopped.
                    And then it dropped,
spring recoiling into body,
into earth's steam-saline lap,
and tremors shook the hollow crack
as, grumbling and vanishing,
its wild heart juddered back.

Lazarus

As slowly he sat up the ache suffused
his whole left shoulder where his life lay bruised,
tearing his death away like gauze, section by section.
Since that is all there is to resurrection.

Revenant

This was the table. Legs and board.
This was the wire. This the lamp.
A glass beside it. Here it is.
The very water that I drank.

From this window I looked out
and saw the crooked dripping mist,
a huge branch in the darkening pool
of the field like a limp wrist.
I looked from the window in the wall
and I had eyes and arms and all.

I'm like a chair-leg now, so tall.
I seem to kneel, so low am I
who cut through space once, shoulder high.
How many birds there were. What space.
Like flowers in a windswept lace
of fire, their petals torn, that sway
and hiss in swarms, or float away
at one great throb and spring apart
like fragments of a bird's blown heart.
There's one explosion and they fly.
And that was fire. And that was sky.

I'm going now. I would
reach to the ceiling if I could.
A low draught blowing where I list
out in the street. I don't exist.

Alcohol

The forest at its death rattle
in tangled knots. The hot
alcoholic flame of summer
gone. Sweep up the lot,

drink it all down. Squeeze out
the rest and fill the bowl.
Go ahead and warm your throat
on its evil, clouded, rotgut soul.

Breath

Do not desert me, air, allow
your servant to breathe deeply now,
let your angelic, silver-dressed
shadows flicker within my chest
like shapes in X-ray images.

Grant me a silver poplar, let
my yearning face be closely set
against it and allow me to
breathe into it and let its breath
continually return my new
unsullied life to me, and float
between our mutual pair of faces
infinities of breathing spaces.

Carbon Dioxide

Plant is the only pure one. Of no school
and ignorant of categories
it is she who in the dark will synthesise
the wicked dioxide molecule.
By morning heaven's tent glows pure and bright
through her transubstantiative work at night.

Like Someone...

Like someone who has brought the news
from far away and then forgot it,
of all those grains of light retaining
a single atom, one small packet –

so those with faulty memories drift
within the body's wrinkled shift.

To a Sleeping Figure

You, anonymous, bare figure,
you who rise from every heap
of silent ash, you occupy
the seventh chamber with your sleep,

not dead but sleeping in your bed
of bark beside an ash-grey wall:
within the room torn curtains fall,
their great unmoving wings outspread.

I do not stir.
Mere states revolve, slow inundations:
sleep images alone remain
turning in unseen constellations.

Wake up! Wake up! Thrust shoulders free.
Though wounded almost mortally
I'll find you yet and talk life out.
Speak, tell me where you've been at last
in dreams you cannot speak about.

Dialogue

– Let go of me, flagstaff! Why cling on to me?
– You're merely rag, dear flag, till you belong to me.

Wind

The distance between columns grows.
Between the words the quick wind blows.

Great cupolas of cloud scud by.
A building plastered down with sky.

Here Nothingness is worth precisely
what fits between the houses nicely.

Bird

On my shoulder squats a bird,
conjoined at birth, our souls allied,
grown so vast and burdensome
I'm racked with pain at every side.

He weighs on me, he weighs and numbs,
I'd shoo him off, he'll not be shook.
He is an oak that sinks its roots,
he digs his claws in me like hooks.

I hear his awful avian heart
drumming at my ear, and know
I'd topple over like a log
if he were now to up and go.

AKHENATON

From the Notebooks of Akhenaton

There must be something I could bring
to bear on this long suffering,
some deity I could invent,
to sit aloft, omniscient.

Desire's no longer adequate:
heaven should be of rough cement.
Therefore, lord, I'll take your weight
and raise you to the firmament
where cherubs will maintain your state.
Once you're up I'll see you right:
you'll not go naked in the night.
Now go and clip this bloody track
of griefs about your waiting neck,
and let it be the lukewarm robe you wear
(your tender plants have ever been my care).
And seal my search for truth behind the doors
of that jewel-encrusted heart of yours.

Enough. Proclaim how good it is,
perform your mighty offices,
sit, stare, eternally, in state.
Begin, it is already late.

The Night of Akhenaton

By the time he reached the open square that night
the tents had been soaked through with lanternlight,
candles were stuck in bottles. It was bright
as summer on this All Souls Day,
and on improvised shelves there lay
crêpe-paper dolls of rose pink thick with dust.

Piled up on one side were tattooed heaps
of oil green melon rinds, their bodies scarred
with heart shapes picked out with old knitting needles.
Above them, neon signs were curling like hair.
A hot wind. Straw in the air.
The night was very dark.

He walked, as if circumscribed
by his presence in some guise,
walked without moving, as a train ran by
on rails above him.
            Wash your face now. Dip your face
      in the bowl of your cupped palms,
      in the basin of your palms
      the will is most where it is least,
      let it drink like a bird,
      let it drink, like beast,
      wash your face now, let the sun,
      each of whose beams terminates
      in one small hand, oh let it run
      its hands across your face –

Night now. And the canvas, growing heavier,
slumped between the pools of light,
between the stalls, which sparkled like boiled sweets
and hung like distant glow-worms, gleaming,
candles suffocated: sudden gusts.

      The old garden.
      Hundreds of thousands in the garden,
      under a sky the colour of wafer,
      it's the other face that must be swallowed,

and the green flower, the Judas tree
he hangs himself on in disgrace,
and the faint green of a star above,
the infinite walked in the garden,
I only wish that you, my love
were as small as the god on the wafer.

And the tanks were already coming.
                    The street ran along
its stone bed before mountainous waves of metal,
and soft bodies ran between stone and metal
still trailing a few balloons behind them,
their flapping canvas of collapsing tents,
the splashing sound of barriers,
distant ashes and fine showers of glass,
and in the silences, whatever blew above them,
whatever blew
above, above the entire planet.
He leapt across some rails along
with all the others,
together they rolled down an embankment,
piecemeal, jerkily, tumbled
under continuous gunfire, over each other
like an avalanche.

*

There was fog by the time he could see again.
He lay on the embankment. A reed.
Another body beside him in the mud,
stretched out so cool, so any old how
you'd think the fresh snow were intended for him.
He left him lying. With a single movement
he rose up, as if he were smoke,
left him lying, or rose up from within him,
and he looked so transparent lying there.
He rose, he lay, it was a single movement.

And was still carrying him, even as he set off.
Still carried the body in the dreaming light.
Through horizontal lines of attenuated mist
he went,
          his left hand wrapped up in his right.

When

In carving myself a god, I kept in mind
to choose the hardest stone that I could find.
Harder than flesh and not given to wincing:
its consolation should appear convincing.

Pure Good

Nor fish nor flesh as good might be...?
Myself, I am no manichee.
Eternal bliss would not, for me,
prove wearisome.

Akhenaton in Heaven

There everything is as it is. The mine.
A mountainside cleft to its heel. The instruments.
As he gently taps the limestone face
dawn shakes, uncertain of its place.
As if it were dawning from within,
the whole cliff like a narrow sheet,
stone and iron transparent now and thin
after ultimate defeat.

There lies the forest.
The fog proceeds in chunks.
Five-fingered, like abandoned hands,
or stretching upward, vertical,
they're tugged along as if by hawsers,
and, failing to gain a meaningful stature, are found
trickling faintly along the ground,
so they proceed,
and so expand or fall in broken ranks,
cloudy, attenuated trunks,
an alternative forest moving between the trees,
billowing mock boughs and shrubberies.

A tunnel there under the trees.
Shady grasses, gravel:
a narrow gauge railway, and now daybreak.
The sun arriving on a head of steam,
slicing the fog neatly, beam by beam,
sun on its way, as its mute rumbling shows,
the metal under the grass sparkles and glows,
the whole morning glows,
while a wall of bushes suddenly rises up,

where the rails have stopped under their grassy bed.
Then only a few sleepers lie ahead,
like halting steps to be negotiated,
and a clearing where the sun stops dead.

It's morning there. Enormous plants.
The camomile field still and solemn,
hoarding a few scraps of iron,
the air above them thick with pollen,
the white spokes of vegetative suns,
unruffled galaxies, no wind whatever.
Noon. For eternity. For ever.

The Objects

Look up to their massed blocks. In noon-light they stand, apart.
The objects are at peace within my heart.

Above the Object

Because the head of every object glows,
trees glisten like arctic circles. In long rows
all 92 elements stand, frozen in endless white,
each wearing its own curious cap of light,
on each one's brow its likeness and reflection –
so body, I trust, shall rise in resurrection.

Love

Good. You're lovely, Nefertiti.
Now I've invented a new deity.

THE SLEEPING HORSEMEN

Night Oak

Night-time: the walker,
hearing a sound, turned round to see
an oak tree in pursuit.

Stopped and waited for it. The oak
proceeded dragging on raw roots
still shedding earth, wriggling long serpentine limbs
down the metalled road,
an awkward mermaid thrusting forward,
its crown too broad, brushing against
silent awnings,
and having reached the night walker
it stopped to lean against the lamp post
push hair aside.
Behind the hair an oak tree's face looked out.

Huge face of moss. Perhaps. Or something like.
The night walker felt his own
contours grow slack,
his dissolving coastline swimming in fog,
like one darkening
in a hidden tarn in a forest,
this was the face he reflected.

Both paused, took breath.

There were birds' nests in the oak's hair,
and in them, sleeping birds, unaware
unremembered.
                    Because the matter was urgent.
It stood there motionless and urgent
like a news item in oak form,
which stales, uninterpreted.

Let fall its curtain of hair.
Turned round. Set off. Strange-footed.

It took its nests and birds
and before the solidifying eyes
of the night walker
neon signs sprinkled light on it,
and melted back into the hole in the ground
which was ready to receive it.

Four Panes of Glass

1

The first is a park.
A garden path between leafless branches,
a garden path, a thick yew tree one side
dotted with tiny winter fruit
glazed *fin-de-siècle* red
and other things,
more details yet – but why?
It is the garden path that marks
this pane, the path like a bird's neck
whose backward arch may be conveyed
by using hands, not words,
stretching its inconceivable avian head
towards the fogged density of the garden.

2

The second pane is misted.

3

The third pane is concrete.
I mean a garage roof
(one sliced in half by the sill, and below it,
invisible, in made to measure
tarpaulin, a selection of creatures,
retracting the lightnings of their lacquered,
polished, chrome surfaces,
hollow cylinders
of silent four-stroke machines
in the viscous chill of winter garages)
and outside, scalding winter suns,
the spotted woodpecker's tropical
spectra caught in the wrong climate,
as it crosses the snowfield
and rounds the horizon
like a steering-wheel, spinning
noon-rings about the flashing sun.

4

The fourth pane is sky,
stretched tight, without creases.
The rare silence of the atmosphere
as it fails to write on thick slate
its inexhaustible cloud dialogue,
one or two lines, no more, broken signs,
attempts at interpretation,
shred, constituent, promise.

The Sleeping Horsemen
(for Lajos Kassák)

December. Noon. A blinding white
snowfield broad as the hill is wide.
On the steep slope a pile of cubic stones.
Over their rounded edges, thin,
a hot white sheet of snow:
a clutch of sleeping bedouin.

Strange faces bent towards the earth
within that dark tight shrubbery,
among inverted statuary!
What dried-up line of black roots tugs
downward within the scree
with hot dark breath for company –

And deep below, below the shore
what kind of bedouin horses stare,
their shapes upwelling here and there,
as down some stable-corridor,
drumming, dumb, invisible,
their great manes like a beard-root bound
billowing freely underground –

And what movement when, sudden, they,
the hot horses of earth and clay,
with all the earth-brown tribes they bear
upon their backs, strain upward with their leafy hair,
and with one slow enormous leap
gallop away.

Hemisphere

Here is the upper hemisphere. Still grey
where grey and watery-white combine
like steps on a staircase recently wet
that with the white turns whiter yet.

Here is the high ground, where the thaw
begins, on low grass glazed with frost,
where dew stitches grass and air
together, so it may reveal
the upper levels of the meadow,
making an uncertain rainbow.

Then suddenly the eye of God
appears in the sky, triangular, quick,
mutating, unexpected trick
of all the lost millennia –
and in that moment turns to metal,
a concave metal altitude,
and draws up the last drops of dew
as it might the spiral trail
of vertigo scrawled on the air,

of all white metals the apogee,
upper half of the world of globes,
the morning's own theology

where one dark half hangs on and aches
like a black cauldron under the great lakes.

Spectacle

The blue. The green. The bed of the stream.
The way things change.
The walls of my skull are plastered with images
like a circular screen.

Even by night they disturb me,
the walls with their night-luminosity,
their bright knives, furniture –
a fern shakes me awake as I lie
with its long-rotted underside
and spores,
like an aerial photograph
of complex city floors –

They're sharp all right, yes, sharp,
every image perfectly sharp,
I'm blinded by the way they mass in herds
coming and going in silence,
tin and grease and birds
in flight without dimension,
planets without electron-shields
driven to high densities,
roots mangled into balls
as they spin infinitely far from us
trapped in an incandescent present
in spaces without intervals.

I live in a tree.
                Its bough has no seasons,
it touches the sky and almost stutters.
I see crowds of husked fruit
gathering.

PROSE POEMS

The Transformation of a Railway Station

Unlikely,
    that there should be earth under all this, here where cobble-stones clad the street like prehistoric fossils. But it seems that under the stones, under the cables, under the intricate lymphatic system (those pulsing installations) there is earth after all, despite everything: there is earth.

A crater now, as it turns out. Or a major surgical incision. On a large rare beast from the zoo, with anaesthetic and outsize instruments. Intestines piled high. Because this body must be dissected, lobe by lobe. The liver and kidneys are separated out. Brutal yet precise movements half way between butchery and healing.

The incision area is sensitive. Tortured houses with peeling stucco, like secondary symptoms of disease. Exhausted trams lurch down ligatured veins, connections tacked together over a shortage of subsiding stones, swollen stitches of rail. And the plants, those ultimately defenceless beings whose stalks they break when they throw them in the bin, as they broke Christ's limbs after taking him off the cross: the dusty terror of plants.

In the middle of all this, the excavation. Diggers with fixed platforms. The operator above like a pilot suspended in mid-air. The astronauts in lemon-yellow rubbers clambering into ditches. Between barriers, the earsplitting racket, the studied calm of catastrophe, the panic of indifference. A plastic bag covering a tangle of wires. (The food-packages of the world. Paper, plastics, the odd piece of waterproof canvas. Textures, knots, dressings. Behold this, oh lordlings, behold that, behold the other.) And some pretty strange hats! A whaler's sou'wester, some form of ritual mask.

Here, we will establish an institutional headquarters. Here, the main hall. Asparagus goes here, notice board there. Look...can you see? Up there, among all those vacant cubic metres, there, yes there, that is where we shall put whatever does not yet exist. It's still transparent, still negotiable. It's a bit draughty up there. A good lens can fix that though. And the appropriate wattage. For it's the merest whisker that forms the barrier between it and ourselves, the merest whisker that prevents it existing. You can practically see its edges above you, hovering between certainty and uncertainty so it is almost ready to be discussed as it swims into your ken like something diminishing put into reverse (a huge hazy ocean liner), pre-existent with all its impenetrable storeys.

You do, of course, remember the railway turntable? The station terminated in an elliptical foundation stone, and at the head of the foundation stone, the steel drum. The engine was parked on it and turned with it like a circus elephant. The old yellow station building is still there with its ancient but still-functioning nostalgias. The lamps behind curls of steam, the dawn rain. And the rails and sleepers at night (you must look at these from above, from the bridge). Those crepuscular angelic ladders into horizontal infinity.

But turn around. Take another look at the building site. (What I mean is that you should try to find your way, among the signs of whatever may be described as event, back to what may be described as presence.) Take a glance at the *Vérmezo*, the Field of Blood. And The Bastion above it. Consider the calm of the wounded, who are used to it. Observe them (in the relationship they used to exist in too), then – even more clearly – take proper account of the curve, as the archaeological dig arranges itself at the foot of the hill. So. Now the picture is focused.

You do, of course, remember when they finished it? Were you there, at the end? Were you also at the opening? It has broadened since then. It is competitive. The escalator wells were not quite...never mind. Track control. Construction company. Junction point.

You do of course remember the lemon-yellow rubbers? The food-packages of the world? The terrain between certainty and uncertainty? You do remember the *Vérmezo*, don't you? The archaeological dig at the foot of the hill? The relationships that once existed? The transformation? The construction company? The airport? You do remember the town?

You were there at the opening, weren't you?

The Proportions of the Street

But those details, the cats. Because it's obvious that the tram leans into the bend like a retired athlete or like the earth on its elliptical orbit: a likeness is not a likeness, but a different aspect of the same law. In other words the relationship between mass and movement – proportions, interdependences, coefficients. This is what you see in the street.

This is what you see when I remove the contingent: the slope of the ecliptic becomes visible, in the morning or at six in the evening, when it's overcast, when the sun is out. If I were to strip the house down, if I were to strip it to the bone, if I were to strip down locomotion (the thing that covers the plants, the dome of the sky), then lines would remain, inflexions, webs. But the web too is only a diagram, the inflexion a form of visual language. The law is invisible. But this is obvious.

And the points of intersection. What I mean is, the points of intersection between that which has life and that which is lifeless. The intersection of two laws. Of three laws. Of sixteen. Their points of intersection. So if I carefully strip away the contingent, I will see the brilliant stars of the intersections, and, extending from them, corridors, condensed bands in the blue of the imagination.

But, as I say: the details, the cats. Compared to the law of course they are merely froth and bubble. Little hairballs to be blown away, wigs bobbing in the flood. The vast deep lies beneath them; the hills and valleys behind. Mountain ranges rucked between watersheds, the geology of the known planets. Underlying them, comparisons and scales, cubic kilometres, ounces, the enormous conical mantle of the earth's shadow in space, centimetres, years, the degrees of heaven; feet, dynes, decibels, Monday, Tuesday; consequences, abstractions.

It's obvious. The world is simply transparent. House and tarmac are transparent: behind them the metallic framework of the scales. They are coming into focus, as in a filmic dissolve, another aspect, another sky.

If I were to strip away the contingent, the blackness of astronomical charts and the night sky's silver landmarks would be visible behind it.

What is the foreground compared to this? The poor man's bible for one thing, image and image, and yet another image; form and what follows it. Painted in neat rows and displayed on the walls of the cathedral. First two little naked figures and the apple, followed by the pretty wings of the angel, the sword twinkling in its tiny fist, followed by flood, ark and peacock, followed by the lamb, followed by Nehemiah. (And behind them, of course, we should not forget the stone wall – the above-mentioned framework, the column with its scales, sometimes so unexpectedly projecting, elbowing its way into the ground-plan of our histories.)

But... But I... One only. Once only. For all that, I would simply like to tell the story of the cat, a single cat of minimal consequence, as it crosses the street, diagonally traversing the limits of measurement as it goes, padding on its four, worn, putty-rubber paws, moving along to the rhythm of its small protuberant shoulder-blades, disappearing (a silent declaration of independence) between the side of a car and the trunk of a lime tree.

It's not there now. There's nothing now. He touches me only from a distance – as a last gesture – with the two lilac leaves of his eyes.

A Walk through the Museum

My only pleasure these days is the museum. The exhibits, the air almost clear of dust, the reflections on the glass of the display cases. The way the attendants, two old women, sit in the corner, their grey hair permed into waves, one of them carefully sipping coffee from the cap of a thermos flask.

I don't really look at anything. Please don't think I'm there to look. I look at nothing. Regrettable but true. Celtic axe-handle, medieval tile, picture, non-figurative statue: I ignore them all.

Or do I look? Have I looked in the past? Looked too much so that all looking is now superfluous? Because I can look at them now, there on the wall opposite, a whole row of living proofs: blues, copper-colours, patches, gradients, the dark-brown charges of night cavalry
    '...tomatoes with cabbage. Simpler.'
    'I used to make it with peas.'
suspended by their spears, driven forward by spears, holding them, vertical, howling as they fling them. Or is it something else? Is this the same set of pictures? Do any of them of match up? Mere references on a wall, quotations from an obsession?

Perhaps this is enough. A picture frame on a white expanse of wall, possibly with a picture in it: it may be enough. It might be a row of broom-handles in the frame, that naive little path leading into the background among trees. The road can take us no further: it is impassable. There is no shoe to tread it, no hoof to gallop it. Not even an aircraft – some small agricultural whirlybird – to flutter clumsily along its curves, cleverly sniffing its way from above. Yet how poignantly the road invites us, with its imperceptibly arcing movement, sucking us, wafting us in, my eyes, the eyes behind my eyes and the eyes behind those eyes (its magnetic field comprising man-made eyes) along lines of force organised into arcs.

Could there be a more relaxing window anywhere in the world? Such a bundle of sunlight on a sunlit-yellow floor? Are there, anywhere in the world, such rough corroded blocks of stone displayed on such polished stands? Do they include such balls of cotton fluff, feathery playthings, just a wee bit dirty. Is there

'Plain one, purl one.'
'Then a blanket-stitch.'
a greater power than that of dawdling down a long series of exhibition rooms, past successive stripes of light – now dark, now bright – air set into columns?

Then to step out of the quasi-colonnade into the square, with a glance from the topmost stair at the lazy panorama in front of you, at the Danube, with neighbourly lines of hills beyond, then slowly meandering down into the smaller landscape of the gothic garden. Into the narrow space between building and battlements, geometrical lilliputian flowerbeds, with tiny round laurel trees beside them: whenever I do this I feel I am stepping into a child's drawing, a Book of Hours with small coloured engravings. I have to move more carefully here, to learn the scale of an existential game. Slowly, warily, ever more narrowly along the path of an enormous mini-universe no shoe can tread. Nevertheless, I must proceed and measure this alternative terrain with steps whose deeds exceed imagination. Breathe slowly and warily. The air has been calibrated into limited quantities.

Whence the shadow on this domain, whence the light? Of course, it is the two chestnut trees there that are the cause, two scarlet-flowered great wild-chestnut trees that glow above me, that act as tents in such a holiday-mood that the hidden otherworld down here is soaked in smoky greenish-reddish light. One must stop. One listens with slightly raised head to something almost audible.

There is nothing left to do now but to leave. Leave the garden by the gate, descend the hill, with the rondella to your left of course, and to the right…to the right the quarry shed with its wire-fenced side where feral cats swarm over miscellaneous old stones. My suggestion would be to take a look at it. See the cats, teeming monuments, squatting on the exhibits, blessing the marble with their little rumps. Their feline stench will follow you, their wonderfully artistic necks turn lazily after you and watch you disappear down the slope.

A Terraced Landscape

When the century fell into step beside me I couldn't quite tell which one it was. There are, undoubtedly, many centuries and which particular one this was, displaying itself in human form, is anyone's guess.

I went along with it, wherever it led. There was a square there. Or a hall. Square or hall, I say – I wouldn't want to lie to you – but in close-up it was clearly an overspill effect of the time-frame. There were forms in the middle of it. They were seated.

As we stepped in front of them, my unknown companion and I, they stood up. Thirty-four centuries stood up, their dark cloth garments rasping as they rose, thirty-four of them – or thereabouts – heavy, some with hoods (though all of them were hooded) carelessly drawn together.

How strange you are, I thought, or not so much strange, I thought, as perfectly natural, I thought, like a flock of water-fowl on a pond in some barren terrain, and now you will fly away, I thought, but they didn't. On the contrary: one by one they followed me, pilgrims, drifting past a line of oil-wells along a horizon that had grown infinite, and so we reached the first level.

The first level.

Or possibly the thirty-fourth, depending on how you look at it, in any case the one furthest from us. The point is that it was a sandy desert. And far, far off, something, a... an object, a small patch of possibility. Riding the intangible narrow waves of the sand – in precise geological pleats – between four empty skyscapes, now fast approaching in close-up: an armchair in the sand. Straight back, studded with precious stones. Hanging from one side of it, the Ureus, sign of the Pharaoh.

The sign of the Pharaoh of El-Armanah of course, the one I loved. I sank the weight of my meditations into the thin face, a personality, a personality sharp and unmistakeable, like the shadow of his head-dress on the ground. The shadow of his head-dress, the blinding Indian-ink black of its shadow, like a letter inscribed for the first time.

But we are leaving. Leaving. We proceed like a line of geese, in single file, moving uphill. One of the hooded figures lags behind, the peak of his little hood dwarfed far below us. My eyes are just about parallel with the edge of the second level. If all this were raised on stilts I would see it from below, like a streetscape from a cellar.

The second level.
                Empty
The third and fourth.
                Empty.
The fifth level.
                Here we find bronze helmets. Above an ancient Mediterranean fort, as in a maquette, a seashore with bronze helmets. I recognise elements of various kinds of riot-gear hard-hats. In these too, if I scratch away a little, I find the rotted remnants of leather lining. Their colours are different – not the same as their surroundings – but their shapes have ripened, become appropriately voluminous. The peak of one bears the figure of a small bronze bird. How it sings! Without its native woods, welded to a disintegrating metal bush (like a blackbird at night, perched on an antenna), it sings with its beak, its feathers, its back. There is in fact no other sound.

The ninth level.
                A sapling forest of sequioas, hardly taller than ordinary pines. You swim in the darkness of pines: are, one might say, lifted by them. Their air is clear as water, as dense as water, round their trunks the rings of two-thousand years – the slow explosion of what is still-to-come expanding in circular waves around the mute log, the irrepressible core.
An ornamental feather under the trees.
Behind us once more, the desert, I can't tell whether it is the same one. For we should bear in mind that this is a series of sand steps, *gradus ad parnassum*, education by terraces – what else could it be? – it is up these stairs, step by diminishing step, our walk takes us. The terraces are furnished. Phenomena, furnishings. One way or the other they are tangible. There is no doubt as to their condition: they are the cumulations of concrete anxieties.

Level zero.

From the negative infinite we arrive at the *origo*. Now time lies not behind but before us. We do it by our own volition, yes, but out of necessity. The point of intersection: suffering. A wind springs up, the breath of being, of wrinkled skin, the weeping navel, a hidden third eye that like a closed wound gazes out of us from our beginnings to our end. Glances, hair flapping in the sky, opalescent gusts.

A thorny twig on the ground, drowning in sand, a tattered rainbow.

Tenth level.

Well, possessions are certainly piling up here. A conical hat with a veil. A nomad's headdress pierced by arrows, a bishop's mitre, vellum. A tiny leather hood to fit a falcon's head, open and closed imperial crowns. An oriental silk scarf, a Viking bullhorn, small hillocks of mortarboards.

Further off, masks made of bark, wood, clay. Flat open flowers for the hair, behind the ear, humid little fireflies of some southern sky.

Level ...een.

Turbans, so many turbans. Velvet beret, bearskin, a swineherd's fur-toque half buried. A coolie hat, an Inca diadem. And a powdered wig of course, a linen kerchief, a moth-eaten sombrero – all caught in mid-movement.

Birettas are also on the move, an eddy of air has caught them up, our feet wade through a mulsh of hats, labour among a sussuration of billowing headgear. An accusing ebb and flow, spasms of a desire for disintegration, above us the swarming of an ever more ragged spiral that had almost succeeded in flying.

Level ...een.

Top hat. Sailor's cap. Little wreaths of forget-me-nots. 13 generals' shakos rolling past. Pith helmet, apple-blossom. A porter's peaked-cap with a numbered tin badge on it. A straw hat for a sicilian mule with two holes for its long ears. A polished fireman's helmet, the copper blazing like a trumpet voluntary. Private mourning-veils in sunlight, black gossamer.

Twentieth level
Or possibly the first, in any case, the next. It seems
as though we're back at the beginning, the place we started from.
I recognise various sorts of riot helmet. It seems I know them, so
I nod at them. Or might they be hair-driers? Gas-masks? Space-
helmets? Suddenly a rain-shrunk beret flies past, I grasp at it, it
must be...ah, never mind. The capering of rabbit-fur pillbox hats.
A coalman's split sack, a stocking mask. Tattered fur, bristle, feather,
insignia, ribbon, hairgrip, comb, lace.
I'd fossick about a little more but the ground continually gives
way. Not that the hoods have diminshed in number, not in the
least. There are as many with me as there were at the beginning.
Whatever. The first sounds of sliding, the ground giving way. They
are leaving. Already they are some distance from me, further up,
diminishing in size. Their progress is itself like an undulating path.
As in an aerial photograph, sliding across the sky, on an upwardly
billowing horizon, there is only one way left, a geological basin.

The twenty-second level, the thirty-first.
There, far away, up
there. Empty. No, there are hats. Hats, I think. Strands of hair, I
think, glances. Appropriately sized, tiny fields of force. Ornamental
ribbon, flowers to tuck behind the ear, helmets, bubbles.
It's no longer possible to see anything. But something is still speaking,
in snatches, breaking up, thickening. Can you hear it? High up
there somewhere, little cupolas towering above each other, forming
a roof for the whole town, with unknown bells inside them.

Earth's Souvenirs

I think I might have compacted. Like the sediments in a mountain, leaping and collapsing: who could separate them? Silurian, Devonian crushed together: ground into residues likely to confused. Then the deposited rocks with sweet traces of lime; snail-shells worming their way through to the top, the tiny architectural capitals of a ruined biological colonnade.

Never mind; compound these with the obligatory flora, plants butting their dense crotchet heads through the stave, signs of the seasons, the way they proceed upward then downward, upward-downward, up to the heights and back down into the depths, on their endless orderly scales. At first they just stammer and try things out, the quarter-tone of a puny dandelion in a playground; then they make a real effort, grow grandiose, plants tumbling forth in variegated green orations, their arias ever the same, ever ariatic. There are occasional variations of course: leaf, flower, root: same, different, same. But who could regret the tautologies of oak trees? I recognise the language of the Tropic of Cancer; it is answered by its twin in the south, nor does the equator itself ever remain silent.

It is pretty hard work, you know, separating the days from each other. To hazard a guess at the date of the month. I watch carefully and eventually I can tell whether it is the asphalt or the snow that is melting; that's only the merest glimmer of a dawning difficulty, it soon clears up. After a fashion, since just now I was minutely examining my five-year-old right knee, with its deep scarlet scab, half the width of my palm, the blue of it as it heals, and the fading iodine-yellow of its hem. All those children's knees with their bruises, contour maps of discoveries.

The lift. Let's not forget the lift. The lift they built as an afterthought, in the tenement courtyard, as it rose and fell, rose and fell in its vertical glass corridor. How it shone! Was it transparent? Lilac? what I mean is that it was glass-coloured, a glimmering throat penetrated by X-rays – rising, falling – a brilliant snack, a tidbit of melody; an occasionally halting crepuscular buzzing between heaven and earth.

When I dismounted from the camel and offered it a piece of pie, it snatched at it with its enormous front teeth. What an ugly great brute of a head it is from close to, but tell me, is there anything more beautiful than the female camel's eye with its long lashes? I tell you, it's what I noticed when I lost my bronze shield in battle; I saw the long untrodden Egyptian sand, and in the sand-sky, the long lashes of that eye as they billowed above me, rising and falling, the eternal gaze of an animal's eye as it looks at you. And that, by the way, is the reason I lost my shield: the straps broke. Many of us lost our shields. The cowhide wears, cracks, and one day you give it a sharp tug, and snap! So snapped the reins of my chariot, so snapped the strap on my skates, so also snapped the strings of my parachute.

They cut off my wavy brown hair, I wear a forget-me-not in my blonde hair, there's a tonsure in the middle of my pale-red hair with a little skull-cap on it, a little round skull-cap fitted over my tonsure, do you remember? That little...yes. Then the clippers applied to my lush black hair, et cetera. All this is mine: hair, knees, my waterproofs, my toga, my silk skirt, my plaster dressing.

No, no. The present is not an island. It is, at least, an archipelago. I parade before you in a long row, in an archipelago – see it from a bird's eye view – down below that enormous blue, the Earth's recurring souvenirs.

LATE POEMS

Snow

1

This downpouring of silence, I
don't even know if I'm hearing it,
this hardly-there snow-pallor, I
don't even know if I'm seeing it

Only the pine tree, only the roof,
outlines on which it falls
as it hesitates at peripheries
brightens and appals

2

Like the roof-ridge of things
the boundary on which it lies
as in some transitional passageway
it falls, falls and solidifies

3

Like something prepared many years ago
like something waiting an age it falls,
falls like something terminal,
on ever-melting seasons falls the snow.

Sequoia Forest

Platonic ideal of pine forest.
Pine forest but ten times greater.

Who knows how far away the branches are:
the only clue is the fact of darkness.

Cool, gigantic trunks,
warm blushes down a fibre-knotted husk
whose pocks suggest a breasted creature,
a breasted deity, whose touch
might be the salvation of your palms
could you but reach above her swollen root.

You sway dizzily in the humid empire,
with its bottle-brown and faint medicinal scent,
and, should the sun find gap enough to peek through,
its glance would mark a shining path that lit
here and nowhere else and answered no known question.

Strange Afternoon...

Strange afternoon, I doubt now whether
I'd felt so dull before or ever
known a distress so dislocated.
I was a child, uncomplicated
by adult terrors. Now I fear
that happy child might reappear.
Have I improved? I might have done.
But it's another scent I'm on,
I'm different. Of that not-me sense
This poem is the evidence.

Sixty-four now...

Sixty-four now. Summer. No use acting
as if this were what I was quite expecting.
Still there's a thaw, a soft appeasement,
a gentle waking up and easement,
this summer of my sixty-fourth commencing.

In the Garden

It's the garden, always the garden
we should remember. Or rather
to wipe the as-if from the as-if-now,
the as-if-it-existed.

A person might in fact believe
the past would fade away. But no,
it vanishes, then reappears,
reappears having completed its orbit,
just like the seasons which sometimes
condense into seed and sometimes extend
down the unmarked highways of space-time,
re-growing according to statistical norms,
to unwritten contractual laws.

It's there that they walk in the garden which is
newly in blossom, by diffused light, down tree-lined paths,
under well behaved titanic trees,
among the serried ranks of lower orders,
among pansies with striated faces,
cute tiger faces really but still
immature, still in their infancy.
A coil of cable resting on a boulder,
the past or future of some installation.

It's there that they walk, those who return walk there,
walk round in circles, during the whole monotonous
journey turning their backs on us,
though sometimes they might turn round to face us,
their faces luminous
as clearings in dense woods,
as current in wet cables,
now blazing, now fading
away on the spiral cables
of time – then returning the way they came,
away, returning, coming:
again, again, again.

This I have seen...

This I have seen (This I have never seen)
Here I have been (Here I have never been)
Perhaps in some other life
I simply stumbled on the scene.

Perhaps in some other life
(Some other dying, possibly)
Wearing veils, I came this way,
Or strayed here quite unconsciously.

Perhaps I never went away,
Have always been here, earth enfolded,
And stand here lost, without direction
In this bloodless resurrection.

Would you believe...

Would you believe it! How the sense of being
can sometimes take wing,
like a boat round whose dark body
the summer sails insist on billowing.

Only a few gusts of wind
shake it unexpectedly as it leans over,
then the sail straightens, and conspiring
with the surface of the water soaks through
time and again, without tiring.

The Empty Sky

The empty sky. The empty sky.
I can't tell what might satisfy.
no more perhaps than a few bars
across the window to stop my eye.

When she looked back...

When she looked back her face had disappeared.
When she looked back.
The masks that she inhabited
dissolved in earth; green, blue and black
in smeary piles of brow and head
the very last time she looked back.

As soon as she had turned away
two wings, her wings,
began to glow beneath the ray,
the purest silver, wings and lungs
which slowly opened as to fly
an inch or so, then closed again
as she breathed out.

I saw it all,
I saw then they belonged, to me,
not others, sadly, but to me:
between my shoulder-blades she flew
like something light had shivered through,
no mask to stunt her backward view.

Concerning God
The gravest of our deficiency-induced diseases

Admit it, Lord, this just won't do. This manner of creation simply will not do. To deposit this brittle eggshell of a world in the solar system, the brittle eggshell of life on earth, and then, to top it all, as if administering a mysterious mode of punishment, to grant it consciousness. This is both too little and too much. This is to lose all sense of proportion, Lord.

Why expect us to cram an entire universe into toy skulls two human hands can compass? Or will you do with us as you do with acorns which you cram with entire oaks?

I wouldn't use a dog as you use me.

Your existence is not so much a scientific as a moral absurdity. To postulate your existence as the creator of such a world is itself an act of blasphemy.

You might at least have refrained from baiting the trap with so many delights. No one forced you to make clouds, or gratitude, or to crown the autumnal acacia with a head of gold. No one asked for the slender, greenish, sweeter-than-sweet taste of being. That sweet-limed twig of yours, Lord – horrible!

Do you know what it's like to feel your blood-sugar sinking? Do you know what that faint small patch of leukoplakia is like when it grows? Do you know what fear is? Or bodily pain? Or disgrace? Can you tell how much electricity a murderer discharges?

Have you swum in a river? Eaten a crab-apple? Have you handled calipers, bricks, small slips of paper? Do you have finger-nails? To scratch the living trees with, to carve nonsense on peeling plane trees with, while

above you the afternoon stretches ahead, on and on into the distance? Do you have an up there? Is there anything above you?

What did I say? Nothing.

Ágnes Nemes Nagy
THE POET'S INTRODUCTION
(1980)

The poems which follow were written by a Hungarian poet. This means that they were born in a rather special medium, that of Hungarian poetry. For though I consider world poetry today more or less uniform, I am nevertheless aware that the poetry of the various nations or groups of poets may be regarded as separate dialects of this uniform, universal language of poetry. Nothing is further from my mind than to theorise about the history of literature; I simply wish to make two observations about Hungarian poetry as a whole. The first is that Hungarian poetry – may God forgive me for the word – is important.

The disadvantage of being important

Hungarian poetry? Is it really important? I'm quite aware of the startling nature of this statement, though I did not make it to startle nor to seem ingenious. It was no mere coincidence that at an international convention a Canadian journalist said to me: 'Are you a poet? Really? I heard that poets in your country are important people.' I had to smile, the sentence summarised so well the sociological position of the Hungarian poet, and what is generally thought about that position. Unworthy representative of a favourable prejudice, I would like to add that in Hungary this sociological importance has been historically determined, and perhaps not only in Hungary, but also among other peoples who have had a difficult history, whose national consciousness and national existence were as often threatened as ours. Since the threshold of modern times Hungarian literature has been the literature of peril. Historical, social, and political role: the poet as commander, agrarian policy maker, dead hero, minister, prison inmate – for centuries, this has been regarded as natural in Hungarian literature. Thus, being a poet has its personal dangers, not to speak of the disadvantage that this all too conspicuous role could bring with it for poetry, sacrificing its actual starting point, poetic quality, for this same role.

Not that we have anything to complain about when it comes to poetic quality. We see poetry as the leading genre of our literature – *hélas*. Yes, this is a most unfortunate fact, since poetry lends itself least to translation. And to this I would like to add a second comment, something I hold to be fundamental for the entirety of Hungarian poetry, and that has to do with the problem of language. This, too, is related to some extent to the importance of poetry as well as to the disadvantages of this very importance; at least, advantages and disadvantages are as indissolubly mixed in it as in the case of its conspicuous social role.

Every language is unique, the Hungarian language is even more unique. If I were a linguist, I would sing hallelujahs from dawn to dusk for having been born a Hungarian and having been given one of the unusual languages of the Finno-Ugrian group at birth. As a poet, however, I am not always rejoicing. The Hungarian language is isolated, the Hungarian language means certain death in world literature. But the Hungarian language lends itself extremely well to poetry. If I were to make a paradoxical argument in favour of this daring opinion, I would insist that Hungarian is so well suited to poetry *precisely because* it is isolated, because its existence in world literature is perilous, because a certain kind of hopelessness is part of its essence – which, of course means hope *vis-à-vis* the ultimate problems of mankind, the constant, centuries (millennia) old experience of living through extreme existential situations. But I do not wish to force this subjective line of argumentation on the reader, I gladly forego subjective proof. Keeping in mind that existential experiences (of all kinds) can infiltrate the means of conceptual communication of a given group of people, here I merely mention a few of the characteristics of the Hungarian language, its agglutination, for example. This has far-reaching consequences in poetry, especially in the 20th century. This is the reason (among others) why 20th-century Hungarian poetry – taking advantage of the language's assonantal riches – is much more rhymed than is usual in most other literatures. As for rhythm, the sharp juncture of the syllables has made it possible for three rhythmic systems to live side by side in Hungarian poetry: one stressed, one quantitative, and one a combination of the two. This unusual feature of the Hungarian language proves without doubt its thorough prosodic sophistication, its rich poetic possibilities.

And this is what is scarcely translatable. So, here we have Hungarian poetry with its unusual features deriving from its unusual language (and cultural situation), characteristics that are generally untranslatable or even should they be translatable, are unimportant in today's world poetry. All poetry is untranslatable, Hungarian poetry is even more untranslatable.

Towards the realm of the nameless

The poems that follow are by a poet, or so I hope. The medium in which they were born (the Hungarian language, Hungarian poetry) characterises them, but not exclusively. I hope that the degree of their untranslatability does not exceed the rather serious difficulties of human communication in general. I hope they have levels of meaning which can be understood in other languages, or – and this would be great luck, indeed – in the prelinguistic or translinguistic domain of human consciousness, the dimension of phenomena as yet unnamed though similar in all of us. This zone, being significant in itself, is even more significant for me with respect to poetry. When I am sometimes asked what I consider to be most essential for the craft of poetry, I usually answer more or less in these words:

> The poet is the specialist of emotions. In practising my craft, it has been my experience that the so-called emotions have at least two layers The first layer carries the known and acknowledged emotions; these have names – joy, terror, love, indignation. There is mutual agreement about their meaning, they have a past, a science, and a literary history. They are the citizens of our hearts. The second layer is the no man's land of the nameless. If I stop at six o'clock in the evening on the corner of Kékgolyó Street (it means, literally, 'blue ball') and see the sunlight's edge falling at a certain angle on the Castle and the olive trees of the Blood Garden cast a shadow a certain way – I am always seized by emotion. This emotion has no name. Yet everyone has stood at some time or other on the corner of Kékgolyó Street. How often I am forced to give a conventional name to nameless emotions! And not only to oil the pedantic logic of mutual agreement. No. I ruin things myself with my uncomprehending perplexity, and spill the nameless something of Kékgolyó Street into a puddleful of autumn melancholy or a vat of historical enthusiasm. And no wonder, for autumn melancholy and historical enthusiasm are citizens of our hearts.
>
> I think it is the duty of the poet to obtain citizenship for an increasing horde of nameless emotions.

By and large, I used to say things of that sort about the nature of poetry because, by and large, that is what I think. But then it is hard enough to recognise our thoughts and emotions, much less find the appropriate name for them. Nevertheless, I think it may be wise to examine more closely and perhaps add to, what I have already said. Like the railway mechanic who at intervals taps the entire underframe of a long train with a hammer, it is not a bad idea to check from time to time our own convictions.

About the emotions

The first sentence of my statement already gives rise to serious suspicion. I assert here that the poet is a specialist of the emotions. Is that so? Is he a specialist, and of the emotions? Let's allow the poor poet to call himself a specialist; there are so many specialists of this and that, why not the poet? After all, he has a certain manual dexterity, he can do tricks with language, he knows about the anapaest; what is more, he can create a whole series of much more complicated Greek metrical feet in his own language if it is suited to such metres; he can translate tens of thousands of lines of verse, if need be, from ancient and modern poets, *et cetera, et cetera.* He certainly knows as much about the language of poetry as a cabinet-maker knows about wood. But whether the word emotion may be employed to accompany the above requires mature consideration. The word itself is taboo, it has long since gone out of use; we fear nothing so much as that caricature of emotion, sentimentality. 20th-century poetry, the avant-garde and recurring waves of avant-garde revivals, the various fads and schools, attacked not only the intellectual faculty, questioning the rational layer of poetry, but in a less spectacular manner also attacked the emotions, the most characteristic aspect of poetry, whose decisive role in lyric poetry went undisputed from time immemorial till the end of the 19th century. It is all the more disputed today. For nearly eighty to a hundred years we have been safeguarding our vocabulary against pathos. Not that emotion does not sneak back into the poem under various excuses and guises: instead of private emotion collective emotion, instead of manifest emotion suppressed emotion, instead of "beautiful" emotion "ugly" and "true" emotion, instead of a complex of related emotions fragments, allusions, visions; instead of pathos irony, and so forth. The most diverse schools of poetry in all parts of the world give some scope to emotion, rather like the schoolmaster who makes allowances for petty mischief or impropriety. In the course of the great devaluations of our age, emotion in poetry has become improper, not only emotion but also the very conception and nomenclature of emotion. There are profound reasons for the anti-emotional, anti-lyric poetry which we 20th-century poets practise, and these reasons point far beyond the field of poetry itself.

And yet, I am not afraid to call the poet the specialist of the emotions. In spite of what I have said above, I consider the domain of lyric poetry to be not unlike the occurrence of the antelope on the earth. Antelopes may roam far from their native ground, but wherever they occur most densely statistically, that is their homeland. The homeland of lyric poetry is the emotion.

(Did I say I was not afraid to pay homage to emotion? Of course I am afraid. I am very much afraid, I shudder to think I might be misunderstood. I am not thinking of *that* emotion, but of *this* one, not the obvious but the controversial one, not the *pre-*, but the *post-*; post-illusion pockets of emotion, typically 20th-century ones as they appear in our poems, because – *malgré tout* – they must make an appearance. Besides, I may not even be thinking of emotion. What I *am* thinking of is merely coloured by the word *disillusion*, but the seed of doubt does not lie in this time-determined colour but in the concept itself. If we call that existential tension of which a poem is born and which it must contain, emotion, then we might as well keep the time-worn adjective, *emotional*, as the adjunct of lyric poetry.)

Layers

It is a lucky thing that the concept of emotion thus safeguarded, or circumscribed with an unsure pen, has several layers. This gives me more scope. Yes, I believe without a doubt that our emotions have at least two layers, known and unknown, inhabited and as yet unconquered provinces. I consider one of the most important tendencies of 20th-century poetry – manifest in so many schools – the intention aimed at the domestication of the realm of the name-less emotions of all kinds. If I understand my own striving well, for me – in poetry today and always – the most essential thing is the epistemological campaign we conduct in the domain of our own unnamed emotions in order to enlarge our awareness. As Rilke wrote, we stand arrested at our borders and grab at things Nameless. Not that I underestimate the importance of the known, more or less available, contents of our awareness. I merely find them inadequate. Our century, this painfully complicated century, has taught us, among other things, that many of the crucial things in our lives happen in domains beyond the senses, among atoms and solar eruptions, nucleic acids, and ozone shields. The significance of what we are incapable of seeing through, in the usual meaning of the term, of what on the anthropomorphous level of our lives we do not know, has greatly increased, and this is as true of scientific knowledge as of the knowledge of self which may be (also) acquired through art. The two of them jointly – knowledge of the world and knowledge of self – despatch poetry on its difficult 20th-century voyage of discovery into the land of the nameless ones.

But I do not mean to equate poetry with epistemology. By knowledge I mean subjective knowledge, tension, shock, recognition, and if we are lucky, catharsis – all those things that the arts can provide. And if they are incapable of providing this, well then, no reasoning and no ideology on earth can excuse them.

Kékgolyó Street

That nameless power source which is the essence of a poem can be approached in various ways. Surrealism approaches it differently than visionary poetry, Rimbaud differently than Eliot, inflated, loud-voiced evocation differently than poetic signal reduced to a minimum. Personally, I like to follow the guidance of objects. Objects carry "news", *sunt existentiae rerum*; if we try to enclose in a poem the being of an object that has somehow touched us *as it is*, then – perhaps – we may capture a corner of a *Ding-an-sich* world sufficient unto itself. And where is the poet to find objects for this purpose? In Kékgolyó Street, for example.

Kékgolyó is a most unusual street. It has houses. Small ones and big ones. While I lived there I was convinced that it lay at the crossroad of enormous powers. Perhaps I was wrong here. Perhaps I was right. If the latter is the case, then we must take it as proof that every (Kékgolyó) street in the world lies at the crossroad of huge powers. I can safely say that I found and experienced wonderful things at this particular location in the world. On one side of the street there was a café with a neon sign, on the other, a blacksmith's shop. The owner of the shop was also a farrier and coachsmith, perhaps the last in the city (the world); they brought the last horses in the city (the world) to him for new shoes. The light-maned draught horses passed by there, among the tall, modern houses, and went through the gate of a crumbling 18th-century manor-house which persisted adamantly among the big city edifices, like a nest in an asphalt jungle. Five small one-storey houses, as they enclosed their own separate intimacy with the help of the stone fence, with the blacksmith's fire in the centre – this is what we saw, the inhabitants of the surrounding big houses, from above and in reduced scale, as in a Brueghel painting. And we saw, besides, the Blood Garden, one-time scene of executions, today a park with the Castle above, eternal reminders of the transmutations of history. Our history, that is, difficult Central European history; yes, we saw the Castle in flames, we saw the bowl of Blood Garden overflow with the ravages of war. And there was much else; I could talk about the small railway station, a cat's leap away, from where the train leaves for Venice on dark, rainy mornings; about the sycamores, the trams, the clouds, the Buda hills on the horizon.

In short, Kékgolyó Street had everything, and I saw many things in time and space if I stopped to linger on the corner at 6 p.m. Even the Kék Golyó was here, the inn sign of the previous tavern, in front of a new tavern. I often scrutinised this old inn sign, if indeed it was the same, for the blue ball had disappeared time and again. It was found each time, if indeed it was the same, and was hung above the tavern door like the badge of some medieval ballgame, if indeed that is what it was. In any case, it is painted a pleasing blue with a touch of gold here and there. If you squint as you look, it appears ocean-blue with continents scattered here and there. I sometime think that this may be the proper way of looking at the lost, then found, Kék Golyó.

Objects

So then, if you pick up a piece of the world – a pebble, a leaf, a discarded distributor plug, a more or less important fragment of the environment – this something may become a transmitter in your hand which broadcasts an unexpected programme. It broadcasts the world, the known and also what is unknown, what is behind our knowledge. This latter channel we do not understand clearly, or else not at all. We have trouble hearing it, like radio stars amidst ordinary radio waves. But poetry is about this before (or after) all; a poem is not exhausted by its content or formal characteristics. Something is left in it which makes it a poem, something it seizes upon from – as I believe – the unknown realms of the psyche. The known components of poem do not explain its ability to radiate.

That is why a poem is such a fascinating object of investigation, much like pitchblende was for Marie and Pierre Curie, because pitchblende's ability to radiate could not be explained by its known components. Though I do not believe that the unknown agent of a poem could be isolated even through the most thorough scientific procedure, I do think that we can regard as a favourable outcome the ideation of what we do not know. The enormous changes and experiments of 20th-century poetry have this as an aim: not only to portray our age but also to get to know its own nature as poetry. And, getting to know poetry (art) is one road to the knowledge of self. Poetry knows something that we, who make poetry, do not. Perhaps it is no more than the effect of the complete as opposed to process, the effect of the ordered as opposed to the unordered, the effect of being raised above time as opposed to being contingent; a certain proportion, a rhythm, an inner state (*Gestalt*), which are, however, able to communicate something previously unknown.

This unknown is communicated to me mainly by objects; that is why I try to relay objects to the reader: a geyser, a branch, the fragment of a statue, a tram, which may bring with them memories of war (war: the fundamental experience of my generation), or the experience of nature (living with nature: one of the threatened nostalgias of modern man), perhaps the myth of an Egyptian pharaoh (the modern myth: a model of our awareness of life). It would therefore be easy enough for me to say that I am what is called an objective lyric poet, in the sense that objects attract me and also in the sense that the objectivity of the lyric tone attracts me. At the same time I could also say that I am attracted by the intense tension which is generated by these objects at the moment when they rise above the general feeling of peril, as expressions or perhaps counterpoints of that endangerment. Because, when all is told, I love objects. Even the threatening ones. How could I put them in my poems otherwise? Objects have a comforting force-field.

However, I wish to stop here. I might say that I hold poetry to be one of the great roads to human cognition, of recognition through the emotions, that I consider our poetic campaigns into the land of the Nameless crucially important, a factor in the spiritual survival of 20th-century man. Furthermore, I might conclude that in getting to know the Nameless, I was principally helped by objects, and that these objects – for this reason, too – are attractive, I might say radiant, in my eyes, like the above-mentioned materials containing radium. But I can go no further. There is a limit to poetic awareness. This is like a dead-end street in a village. Not a dead end in a city, but one by the outskirts of the village when the asphalt road turns into a rocky road, the rocky road into a mule track, and the mule track simply comes to an end. There is no more road. But though the road is no more, the countryside continues: there are bushes, groves, hills, fields. A lovely wide panorama stretches before us, and the smallest country rabbit, or even a grasshopper, can leap into this roadless panorama: we alone, bipeds that we are, are left stranded at the end of the road and cannot go on. Our reflection does not go on, but the poem does. Reconnoitring the roadless terrain is its speciality. Let us allow the poem to take the leap forward.

Translated by J.E. Sollosy

'The Poet's Introduction' first appeared in *Ágnes Nemes Nagy: Selected Poems*, translated by Bruce Berlind (Iowa Translations, University of Iowa, 1980) and is here republished in a slightly modified form by kind permission of the translator, following the same text as *Between: Selected Poems of Ágnes Nemes Nagy*, translated by Hugh Maxton (Dedalus Press, Dublin / Corvina, Budapest, 1988).

www.ingramcontent.com/pod-product-compliance
Lightning Source LLC
Jackson TN
JSHW011941131224
75386JS00041B/1498